Pets

Amanda Benjamin

CONTENTS

Collins *Children's Books*

your pet

A pet is for ever. With love and good care, your pet will be happy and healthy, and you will have great fun together. Animals need fresh food and water every day and a clean, comfortable home. Although they can't talk, they can show you how they are feeling.

Dogs

Dogs come in all shapes and sizes.

They love to play, and will join in with your games.

Dogs make great friends... with anyone!

4

You will soon learn to tell whether

your pet is

healthy or unwell.

Find out as much as you can

about him or her, and then

spend lots of time

getting to know

each other. You're both in for a treat!

But...

They need walking every day – rain or shine...

...and regular grooming.

Puppies are very lively – and are always getting into mischief!

5

Cats

Cats are full of character.
They are curious, clever
and quick on their feet.

Kittens are
always
making
you laugh.

You can relax with your
cuddly, furry friend...

...or have great fun
stalking through the
jungle with
your very
own tiger!

But...

Pong!

Cleaning your cat's litter tray is a messy, smelly job.

Cats don't always want to play when you *do*.

With love xx

Watch out for unexpected presents!

Rabbits and Guinea Pigs

Rabbits and guinea pigs are easy to look after.

They are friendly animals and if you are gentle they enjoy being petted.

You can house-train your rabbits if you want them to live indoors!

But...

You need to clean out the
hutches often and let your
rabbits out to run around.

Male rabbits or guinea
pigs sharing a hutch will
sometimes fight.

Say
lettuce!

And a male and female will
breed like, well... rabbits!

Ponies

There is nothing as exciting as riding your own pony.

Taking part in gymkhanas is great fun.

Ponies come small enough for the smallest rider.

But...

Ponies can be very cheeky and
enjoy giving you a good run before
you get your ride!

And keeping a pony is HARD WORK...

...what with
grooming them...

...and mucking out!

...cleaning and
polishing
the tack...

Fish

Fish are beautiful to look at and there are hundreds for you to choose from.

An aquarium is like having a lovely moving painting.

With time and care you might be able to train your fish to jump for its food!

You can keep adding to your collection.

But...

You can't take your pet fish for a walk.

Beware! You may
have a bully in
your tank.

You will need to clean
your tank and water
filter regularly.

13

Birds

Birds are always singing and chirping.
They make fun pets.

You can teach
your bird to fly
to your hand...

...and sit on your shoulder.

You can even teach
some birds
to speak!

The rain
in Spain...

...stays
mainly in
the plain.

But...

If you leave
the cage
door
open...

...your bird will   fly away!

A bored bird may
peck and hurt
you, so make
its cage
exciting!

Birds can also
be very messy!

Hamsters

Hamsters are full of energy and love to play.

They wash and groom themselves, and are quite happy being an only pet.

You can have great fun making an activity centre for your hamster and finding new toys for him or her.

But...

If you allow the cage to become dirty, you will soon have a very sick hamster!

Hamsters may be unfriendly at first and need time to learn to trust you.

These pets prefer playing at night!

Rats, Gerbils and Mice

You can have hours of fun with these adventurous pets.

Rats are very clever and can learn all kinds of tricks.

$E=mc^2$

If you go on holiday, it is easy to give your pets to a friend to look after, as long as you tell them what to do.

But...

Gerbils can catch colds and flu from people so you can't go near them when you're ill.

If your pet escapes, it may get lost or hurt...

...and can cause a lot of damage.

Tortoises

Is it Spring yet?

Tortoises are unique creatures – they carry their homes on their backs.

Tortoises can live for a long, long time.

But...

Your pet tortoise will hibernate for half the year and then you won't see it.

Wakey!

Terrapins

Terrapins live half in and half out of the water and like their home to be kept nice and warm.

But...

They can outgrow their tank!

Sometimes they bite and can pass on disease!

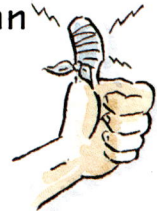

Ants, Spiders and

Insects and spiders are easy to find and feed. You can keep them in a cardboard box or a glass container, and they are fascinating to watch.

An ant house is easy to make.

food
container

bowl of
water

piece of string

Plasticine squeezed
between two sheets
of glass or plastic

drinking
straw

Silkworms
But...

Spiders and ants can be tricky to catch, so why not just go outside and watch them in the wild?

Not everyone likes creepy-crawlies.

Pet insects can easily be thrown away by mistake.

Index

THE BLUE CROSS

If you want information on how to look after your pet or where you can adopt a pet from
The Blue Cross contact The Information Officer at The Blue Cross, Shilton Road, Burford Oxon. OX18 4PF.
Telephone enquiries: 01993 822651. E-Mail: 100677.364@compuserve.com

Edited by Helen Mortimer
Designed by Mei Lim

First published in 1996 by HarperCollins Children's Books,
A Division of HarperCollins Publishers Ltd,
77–85 Fulham Palace Road, London W6 8JB
Copyright © HarperCollins Publishers Ltd 1997

ISBN: 0 00 197965 5

Illustrations : Alan Baker, Mei Lim

A CIP record for this book is available from the British Library

Printed and bound in Hong Kong